Chief Joseph
of the Nez Percé

A Photo-Illustrated Biography
by Lucile Davis

Content Consultant:
Allen P. Slickpoo Sr., Ethnographer
Culture Resource Program
Nez Percé Tribe

Bridgestone Books
an imprint of Capstone Press

Facts about Chief Joseph

- Chief Joseph's Nez Percé name was Hin mah to ya lat k'it. It can mean Thunder Emerging from the Mountains.
- He became a Nez Percé chief in 1871.
- He met three U.S. presidents in his lifetime.
- He never signed a treaty giving up his people's land.

Bridgestone Books are published by Capstone Press
818 North Willow Street, Mankato, Minnesota 56001 • http://www. capstone-press.com
Copyright © 1998 by Capstone Press • All rights reserved • Printed in the United States of America

Library of Congress Cataloging-in-Publication Data
McAuliffe, Bill.
    Chief Joseph of the Nez Perce: a photo-illustrated biography/by Bill McAuliffe.
    p. cm.
    Includes bibliographical references and index.
    Summary: The story of the Indian leader who tried but failed to get his people into Canada in 1877 so that they would not be sent to a reservation.
    ISBN 1-56065-570-4
    1. Joseph, Nez Percé Chief, 1840-1904--Juvenile literature. 2. Nez Percé Indians--Kings and rulers--Biography--Juvenile literature. 3. Nez Percé Indians--History--Juvenile literature. [1. Joseph, Nez Percé Chief, 1840-1904. 2. Nez Percé Indians--Biography. 3. Indians of North America--Biography.] I. Title.
E99.N5J856   1998
979'.004974--dc21
[B]
                      97-3360
                      CIP
                      AC

Photo Credits
Archive Photos, 4, 8, 18; Corbis-Bettman, 6, 16; Idaho State Historical Society, 10, 12, 20; Montana Historical Society, cover, 14

Table of Contents

Native American Leader

Chief Joseph was a great leader of the Nez Percé. The Nez Percé are a group of Native American people. Chief Joseph worked his whole life to protect his people. He tried to avoid war.

In the late 1800s, the U.S. government wanted more land. It tried to make the Nez Percé leave their land. Chief Joseph tried to keep his people's land. But the army forced the Nez Percé to leave. The Nez Percé went to war with the U.S. government.

Chief Joseph was a wise leader. He and his people won many battles against the U.S. Army. The U.S. Army and the Nez Percé suffered greatly. Many of them were killed. After three months, Chief Joseph finally surrendered. Surrender means to give up.

Chief Joseph was also a famous speaker. He gave many speeches about the unfair treatment of the Nez Percé. People still remember many of Chief Joseph's words.

Chief Joseph was a great leader of the Nez Percé.

The Nez Percé People

Explorers gave the Nez Percé people their name. In French, Nez Percé means pierced nose. The Nez Percé received this name because some of them wore shells in their noses.

The Nez Percé lived in one area for hundreds of years. This area was where Idaho, Washington, and Oregon now meet. It is home to fish and wild game. Many kinds of edible roots, plants, and berries grow there, too. Edible means able to be eaten.

The Nez Percé had great respect for the land. They lived mostly by fishing and hunting. The men rode and trained horses. The women made baskets and gathered nuts and berries.

The first white people came to the area in 1805. The Nez Percé were friendly to them. They traded goods with the white people. The Nez Percé also helped them find their way across the country.

The Nez Percé helped the white people find their way across the country.

Young Joseph

The Nez Percé were made up of about 70 bands. One band lived in the Wallowa Valley. This valley is in what is now Oregon. In the mid-1800s, the chief of this band was Old Joseph.

Old Joseph and his wife, Khapkhaponimi, had a son in 1840. His name was Hin ma to yah lat k'it (HIN-MAH-TOE-YA-LAHT-K'IT). It can mean Thunder Emerging from the Mountains. White people called the boy Young Joseph.

Young Joseph grew up in the Wallowa Valley. He had two brothers and two sisters. Young Joseph's father taught him how to hunt.

In 1855, the Nez Percé signed a treaty with the U.S. government. A treaty is an agreement between governments or groups of people. The Nez Percé agreed to give some of their land to white settlers. A settler is someone who moves to a new place.

Chief Joseph's name was Hin ma to yah lat k'it. It can mean Thunder Emerging from the Mountains.

A New Leader

Gold was found on Nez Percé land in 1860. More white settlers came. In 1863, the U.S. government told the Nez Percé to move. It wanted the Nez Percé to live on a small reservation in Idaho. A reservation is land set aside for Native Americans to use.

Many bands agreed to leave. Old Joseph and some other chiefs did not. He said he would not give up his people's land.

Old Joseph died in 1871. Young Joseph became Chief Joseph. The new Chief Joseph tried to work with the government. But he also believed his people should keep their homelands. He refused to sign any treaty giving up his people's land.

In 1877, the U.S. Army ordered all the Nez Percé to move to Idaho. The Nez Percé had 30 days to leave. Some wanted to fight for the land. Chief Joseph knew that many Nez Percé would die in a war. So he agreed to move his people to the reservation.

Chief Joseph refused to sign any treaty giving up his people's land.

War Begins

Chief Joseph's band began their journey to the reservation in May 1877. Four other bands of Nez Percé joined them. Some bands wanted to fight a war. But Chief Joseph tried to make peace.

One night, a few Nez Percé warriors attacked some settlers. They killed three white men. Chief Joseph knew this would start a war. The other chiefs wanted war. Chief Joseph felt he had to join them. The Nez Percé War began.

Chief Joseph knew the army would come after them. He led his people to White Bird Canyon in Idaho. Army soldiers attacked them there on June 17, 1877. The Nez Percé fought bravely and won the battle. Not one Nez Percé was killed.

The Nez Percé fought more battles with the army. They set up camp on the Clearwater River in Idaho. Chief Joseph called a meeting of the five bands. They decided to travel to Canada. The army could not attack them there.

Chief Joseph led the Nez Percé to White Bird Canyon in Idaho.

Crossing Montana

The army chased the Nez Percé. But the Nez Percé escaped the army many times. They moved quickly over mountains and canyons. They crossed through much of Montana.

The Nez Percé were tired, but they kept moving. People all over the United States heard about Chief Joseph's brave leadership.

In August 1877, the Nez Percé camped by the Big Hole River in Montana. The U.S. Army attacked them there. Eighty Nez Percé were killed. Chief Joseph led most of the women and children to safety.

The Nez Percé kept going. They passed through Yellowstone National Park in late August. The army tried to trap them there. But Chief Joseph led his people to safety again.

To escape the army, Chief Joseph led the Nez Percé across much of Montana.

The Run for Canada

The Nez Percé moved north toward Canada. They hoped the Crow people of Montana would help them. The Crows also were a group of Native Americans. But the Crows wanted the Nez Percé's horses. So they helped the U.S. Army.

On September 13, the Nez Percé fought army soldiers at Canyon Creek in Montana. The Nez Percé fought well. They kept moving toward Canada. Other Native Americans had escaped into Canada a year before.

By this time, the Nez Percé were tired and weak. They had traveled 1,300 miles (2,080 kilometers) in three months. About 250 Nez Percé warriors had fought 13 battles with the U.S. Army.

Chief Joseph led his people to the Bearpaw Mountains in Montana. They camped there on September 29, 1877. Canada was just 40 miles (64 kilometers) away.

The Crow people would not help the Nez Percé.

The Surrender

The Nez Percé rested for one day. They thought the army was far away. The next day, 400 soldiers arrived.

Colonel Nelson Miles asked Chief Joseph to surrender. He would not. The Battle of the Bear Paws lasted five days. It was snowing. The Nez Percé dug pits and hid in them. They tried to keep warm.

Many Nez Percé were killed in the battle. Colonel Miles wanted them to surrender. He said they could return to the Idaho reservation. Chief Joseph did not want any more suffering. He was tired of fighting. On October 5, 1877, the Nez Percé surrendered. Chief Joseph gave a famous speech. He said that he would fight no more.

The army broke its promise. The Nez Percé were not allowed to live in Idaho. Instead, the army took them to Fort Leavenworth in Kansas. It was a dirty swamp. The Nez Percé were not used to the hot weather. Many became sick and died.

Colonel Nelson Miles asked Chief Joseph to surrender.

Final Years

Chief Joseph tried to help the Nez Percé. He talked to the army leaders. The Nez Percé were moved to a better place in Oklahoma. But Chief Joseph always claimed that the Nez Percé still owned the Wallowa Valley.

Chief Joseph had become a famous leader. He went to Washington, D.C. to meet with President Rutherford B. Hayes. There he spoke at a meeting of law makers. He told them the story of the Nez Percé.

In 1883, the army returned a few Nez Percé to the Idaho reservation. About 100 others went to Idaho the next year. In 1885, Chief Joseph and 150 others were sent to a reservation in Washington. Chief Joseph died there on September 21, 1904. The reservation doctor said he died of a broken heart.

In his time, many people thought of Chief Joseph as a great wartime leader. Today, he is seen as a man of peace. He was forced into war.

In 1904, Chief Joseph died on a reservation in Washington.

Words from Chief Joseph

"I am tired of fighting. Our chiefs are killed. . . . It is cold, and we have no blankets. The little children are freezing. . . . Hear me, my chiefs! I am tired. My heart is sick and sad. . . . From where the sun now stands, I will fight no more forever."

From Chief Joseph's surrender speech on October 5, 1877.

"If the white man wants to live in peace with the Indian, he can live in peace. There need be no trouble. Treat all men alike. Give them all the same law. Give them all an even chance to live and grow. All men were made by the same Great Spirit Chief. They are all brothers. The earth is the mother of all people, and all people should have equal rights upon it."

From Chief Joseph's speech to law makers in Washington, D.C., in January 1879.

Important Dates in Chief Joseph's Life

1840—Born in the Wallowa Valley in what is now Oregon

1855—Nez Percé sign treaty giving up some of their land

1860—Gold is found on Nez Percé land

1863—Some bands sign treaty giving up most of Nez Percé land

1871—Old Joseph dies; Young Joseph becomes chief of his band

1876—Meets with U.S. Army; refuses to give up land

January 1877—Ordered to move his people to an Idaho reservation

May 1877—Agrees to move to reservation

June 1877—Nez Percé War begins

June–September 1877—Leads Nez Percé on a 1,700 mile journey; the Nez Percé fight 13 battles against the U.S. Army

September 30, 1877—Battle of the Bear Paws begins

October 5, 1877—Surrenders to Colonel Miles

November 1877—Army takes Nez Percé to Fort Leavenworth, Kansas

1879—Visits president in Washington, D.C., and makes speech to law makers

1885—Nez Percé sent to reservation in Washington

1904—Dies on September 21 on a Washington reservation

Words to Know

reservation (rez-ur-VAY-shuhn)—land set aside for Native Americans to use

settler (SET-luhr)—someone who moves to a new place

surrender (suh-REN-dur)—to give up

treaty (TREE-tee)—an agreement between governments or groups of people

Read More

Freedman, Russell. *Indian Chiefs*. New York: Holiday House, 1987.
Osinski, Alice. *The Nez Perce*. Chicago: Children's Press, 1988.
Rothaus, James. *Chief Joseph*. Mankato, Minn.: Creative Education, 1987.
Sherrow, Victoria. *The Nez Perces*. Brookfield, Ct.: Millbrook, 1994.
Sneve, Virginia Driving Hawk. *The Nez Perce*. New York: Holiday House, 1994.

Useful Addresses and Internet Sites

The Nez Perce Historical Park
Route 1, Box 100
Spalding, ID 83540

Museum of American History
Smithsonian Institution
Washington, DC 20560

Chief Joseph, Nez Perce
http://www.indians.org/welker/joseph.htm
People in the West: Chief Joseph
http://www.pbs.org/weta/thewest/wpages/wpgs400/w4joseph.htm

Index